The Mark of God and Our Education Crisis

BY RUSS GREGG

Unless the LORD builds the house,
those who build it labor in vain.
Unless the LORD watches over the city,
the watchman stays awake in vain.

Psalm 127:1

"Then God said,
'Let us make man in our image,
after our likeness...'
So God created man in his
own image, in the image of God
he created him; male and
female he created them."

GENESIS 1:26-27 (ESV)

Introduction

For many years I have called the kind of education we seek to provide at Hope Academy *imago Dei* education. *Imago Dei* is Latin for the image of God, and we also call it education for image-bearers.

It is essential to flesh out more clearly what we mean when we say, "The hope of Hope Academy is God." This is crucially important because people often ask me, "What could schools learn from Hope Academy even if they don't care a whit about God?" I just shake my head. I know I need to do some better teaching.

What I first need to correct is the false idea that schools like Hope Academy are basically doing the same thing that public and charter schools are doing, only we're executing a little better than they are. We're like Avis. We try harder.

No, no, no, no.

Let me assure you, we are not doing the same thing as other schools in our city. We are doing something completely different. We are doing education for image bearers, and there is a world of difference between the two.

Here I will share how *imago Dei* education provides a critical solution to our education crisis, and share some of the story of how God called us to start Hope Academy.

My prayer is that God might use what He has done in our midst to inspire others to take a similar step of faith.

1.
The Crisis
of Honor

1

The genesis of my thinking about *imago Dei* education is really two-fold. The first motivation came from trying to understand the bewildering crisis of honor in our country that is crippling our day-to-day lives, and the second came from reading a powerful quotation from C.S. Lewis' magnificent essay, *The Weight of Glory*.

I think we can all agree that we are suffering from a crisis of honor in America that is crippling our day-to-day lives. From the coarseness of our speech on the airwaves and on social media, to the cheapening of human life, especially the lives of the unborn, to the unwillingness to even listen to, much less consider the merits of an opposing argument, to the political gridlock that is paralyzing St. Paul and Washington, DC. What is behind all this? What's changed?

I believe that the wholesale rejection of the doctrine of creation has resulted in a blindness to seeing and honoring the image of God in one another. Whether we realize it or not, we see one another today as less and less human. Mere material beings don't necessarily deserve respect and honor, do they? Random collections of atoms cannot be said to have any ultimate purpose or sense of dignity.

The tragic loss of the image of God in our society has powerfully affected our schools as well. Q It is no mere coincidence that education divorced from the image of God has relatively quickly deteriorated into the dismissal of God from classrooms, the rejection of truth from textbooks, the disregarding of parents, the abuse of teachers, and the warehousing of students. It has contributed to school shootings, voluntary segregation, a yawning achievement gap, gender confusion, classroom chaos, and now generation after generation lost to drugs, gangs, and teenage pregnancy.

Could the loss of the image of God explain, according to a recent series of articles in the Star Tribune, why black families are fleeing district schools and searching for alternatives in massive numbers?

Thankfully, there is hope in God. The solution to a great many of our city's problems lies in our society's recovery of seeing the image of God in one another, which brings me to that special quote from Lewis's magnificent essay, *The Weight of Glory*. Lewis writes:

> It may be possible for each of us to think too much of his own potential glory hereafter; it is hardly possible for him to think too often or too deeply about that of his neighbor.

> The load, or weight, or burden of my neighbor's glory should be laid daily on my back, a load so heavy that only humility can carry it, and the backs of the proud will be broken.

Q: Have you experienced how this tragic loss has affected school classrooms?

It is a serious thing to live in a society of possible gods and goddesses, to remember that the dullest and most uninteresting person you talk to may one day be a creature which, if you saw it now, you would be strongly tempted to worship, or else a horror and a corruption such as you now meet, if at all, only in a nightmare.

All day long we are, in some degree, helping each other to one or other of these destinations.

Remember, there are no ordinary people. You have never talked to a mere mortal.[1]

Bearing the burden of my neighbor's glory is easier to say than to practice, isn't it? Q It's something that I have struggled with for a long time.

---

1. C.S. Lewis, *The Weight of Glory* (HarperOne, 2001), pp. 45-46

Q: Do you find yourself stirred by the call to help
'bear the burden of your neighbors glory'?

"Remember, there are
no ordinary people.
You have never talked
to a mere mortal."

C.S. LEWIS

2.
Who Is My Neighbor?

2

In 1991, my wife, Phyllis, and I were looking to buy our first home in Minneapolis. We were in our early thirties and starting a family. Along with other friends, we began to ask ourselves: If followers of Jesus are called to be the light of the world, what part of our city was most in need of the light of the gospel? Maybe we should move there to seek the welfare of the city. Q

Everyone in Minneapolis knew there was one neighborhood almost nobody wanted to live in: the Phillips Neighborhood. For decades this neighborhood has been known for two things—extreme poverty and violent crime.

Home to 17,000 residents, most of us in the Phillips Neighborhood don't own our homes. We rent them. 80% of us rent from month to month, and most of us move several times a year. Half of us in the neighborhood live below the federal poverty level. Back in 1996, when over forty homicides occurred in one year, state troopers were sent into the area to patrol our streets.

Q: Is God calling you to live and serve in a hard place in your city?

Today, our neighborhood has changed, but much remains the same. Each Monday I receive an email from the Commander of the Third Precinct, outlining the arrests made during the previous week within a four-block area around our school. Last week there were 20 drug arrests, 25 arrests for prostitution, and three robbery suspects were arrested. On top of this, Phillips has the highest concentration of registered sex offenders living in it of any neighborhood in the state. And in the last month there were three homicides within a four-block radius of the school.

When my father heard that we were buying a house in Phillips he said, "Russ, you're an idiot! Everybody knows that you buy a house as an investment. Your investment is going to decrease in value every year. You're going to be paying an annual tax for the *privilege* of living in Phillips." But against his advice, 26 years ago, we bought our home three blocks from here. We still live there today.

"But seek the welfare of the city where I have sent you into exile, and pray to the Lord on its behalf, for in its welfare you will find your welfare."

JEREMIAH 29:7 (ESV)

3.
Our Neighbors
& the Education
Crisis

3

As our children became school age, my wife and I began to understand that the poverty and crime in our neighborhood had a deeper root. There was an education crisis in our neighborhood of which I was completely ignorant.

Soon I learned that:

- Over half of my neighbors were not going to graduate from high school.
- Those neighbors who did graduate from high school would, on average, read at only an 8th grade level.
- The state of Minnesota, often known as 'the education state', had the largest Achievement Gap between white and non-white students of any state in the country, which meant that my non-white neighbors were getting one of the worst educations in the whole country.
- I discovered that many of the boys who were not reading proficiently by 3rd grade were likely going to spend some time in prison.

This crisis is nationwide. In 2010, when filmmakers made a documentary about this national urban education crisis they called it "Waiting for 'Superman.'" I'm not aware of any other problem facing our country where leaders have felt so hopeless that they've started calling upon superheroes for help.

Like all parents, my wife and I wanted a great education for our own kids.

So, what did we do when they became school age?

We drove our kids ten miles across town to attend a great Christian school in the wealthiest neighborhood of our city. This solution created a massive problem for us. We had moved into Phillips to be a light to our neighbors, and we were now forced to ask ourselves another disturbing question: What does it mean to really love your neighbor as yourself? Wanting to justify myself, like the expert in the law whom Jesus had told to love his neighbor, I asked myself, "And who is my neighbor?"

"And he answered,
'You shall love the Lord your God
with all your heart and with all your
soul and with all your strength
and with all your mind, and your
neighbor as yourself.' And he
said to him, 'You have answered
correctly; do this, and you will live.'
But he, desiring to justify
himself, said to Jesus,
'And who is my neighbor?'"

LUKE 10:27-29 (ESV)

Let me tell you about what life is like for Jasmine,[2] a teenage girl living on my block. Jasmine typically misses one to two days of school each week, and when she goes to her neighborhood school, she's often exhausted because she's awakened by sirens and gunshots fired around her apartment. She and her Mom and her two younger brothers moved twice last year. They hardly have any furniture in the apartment: No art on the walls; only a kitchen table and a mattress on the floor; and the few personal things Jasmine has are still in a box from last month's move.

Her Dad is in prison, and her Mom works two part-time jobs, one during the graveyard shift. Since her Mom sleeps in the morning, Jasmine has to get her brothers up herself and get them ready for school. Sometimes there's no food in the refrigerator or the cupboards. But she and her brothers get breakfast and lunch at school.

School is a pretty chaotic place. She says there are fights in the halls almost every day, and her classmates swear at the teachers. Nothing is ever really done about it. She says that she is often offered drugs at school.

Jasmine is not on track to graduate. She doesn't understand what's going on in math class—she hasn't for years—so she doesn't do the homework anymore. Nobody at school seems to really care anyway.

Jasmine is struggling with depression. An uncle sexually abused her a few years ago.

Jasmine wants to play on the basketball team but her mom said she can't

---

2. The name and some details of this neighbor have been changed to honor her privacy.

because she has to take care of her brothers after school. She can't risk taking them outside to the park to play because it's not safe. She's never been on a family vacation. Never even visited Minneapolis suburbs like Woodbury or Eden Prairie, though she's heard about them and wonders what they're like. If she's like most of her friends, Jasmine will probably have a child and drop out of her high school before graduating.

Jasmine is our neighbor.

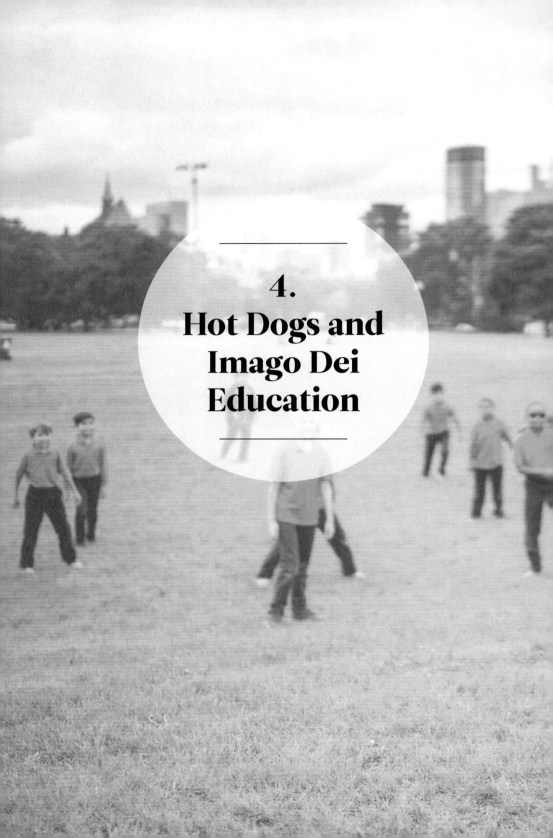

4.
Hot Dogs and Imago Dei Education

4

So what could it mean to recognize the *imago Dei* in Jasmine and love her as I love myself? The meaning of the image of God in the Bible is rich and varied, and there are many models commentators have used to seek to understand it. Dr. John F. Kilner, in his recent book, *Dignity and Destiny: Humanity in the Image of God*, comes to a very compelling conclusion on the subject.

Referencing 2 Corinthians 4:4 and Colossians 1:15, he argues that the image of God is not primarily found in the interior of our bodies, or in our rational or creative powers. Instead, the image of God *is* Jesus Christ.

"We are not the image of God. Christ is the image, and all humanity has been *created in his image*," says Kilner. "The preposition 'in' more specifically means 'according to.' So God created people *according* to his image, which is Jesus Christ. Christ is the standard, the model for what a human being should be." [3]

---

3. Quoted in Tony Reinke, "In the Image of God We Trust," desiringGod.org. Nov. 5, 2016.

The *imago Dei* means that all humanity, more than anything else in all creation are uniquely made to reflect and display the greatness of God. How should this impact the approach we take to education? Let me give you an example.

Almost every month a different church or ministry group comes into Peavey Park in the Phillips Neighborhood and serves a meal to the poor. Can you guess what's usually on the menu? It's almost always hot dogs.

Now there might be a place for this sort of short-term mercy outreach. However, we are all too comfortable with offering a "hot dog kind of education" to our neighbors — even though we would never accept that kind of education for our own kids. If I want a "filet mignon education" for my own kids, wouldn't Jesus encourage me to desire that same kind of education for Jasmine?

But that kind of love would be so costly.

Like the priest in the Good Samaritan story, for six straight years, each morning I put my kids in the back seat of our car, and I drove right around my neighbor's children as I took my own kids to school.

I often waved, and sometimes in frustration, I would shoot up a prayer and ask God to "tell someone to do something about this problem." Q

The Lord must have often smiled and said, "Well there is this one guy named Russ that I've put there, but he's got two big problems. First, he's got a hard head, but you know what's even worse, he's got a hard heart."

Q: Have you prayed similar prayers for a Christ-centered education for your neighborhood?

"'Which of these three, do you
think, proved to be a neighbor to the
man who fell among the robbers?'
He said, 'The one who showed him
mercy.' And Jesus said to him,
'You go, and do likewise.'

LUKE 10:26-27

5.
Rejecting Three Specific Lies

5

Looking back, I now see that I sinned against my neighbors by believing three specific lies related to God's purposes for my neighbors.

First, I believed there was some kind of cash flow crisis in heaven and that the maker of heaven and earth certainly couldn't provide the millions of dollars it would take to provide a remarkable school for my neighbors.

Second, I believed the lie that the fear of men was of greater value than the approval of God.

And lately, I've come to see that I also succumbed to an insidious third lie — that there are different levels or degrees of the image of God in different peoples.

At a subconscious level, I justified my indifference to the educational needs of my neighbors by believing the lie that my African-American, Latino, and Somali neighbors were less deserving of a God-centered education than my own kids.

Where did that kind of implicit bias and racialized thinking come from? I had always thought I believed that all men were created equal, but as a child, different messages were sent to me.

For instance, my family lived in the wealthy suburbs outside Milwaukee, but my Dad owned a bar and restaurant within the Milwaukee city limits. Often he would put us in his Cadillac and drive the family to the restaurant. As we passed from a predominantly white part of the city to a predominantly black part, I would always hear a loud click—the sound of the power door locks locking the car.

Though we never spoke about this, the implicit message sent to me was that people here are not like us. The truth of the *imago Dei* teaches us that that's a lie. And even though I've walked with God for 35 years, I'm still repenting of that kind of false thinking.

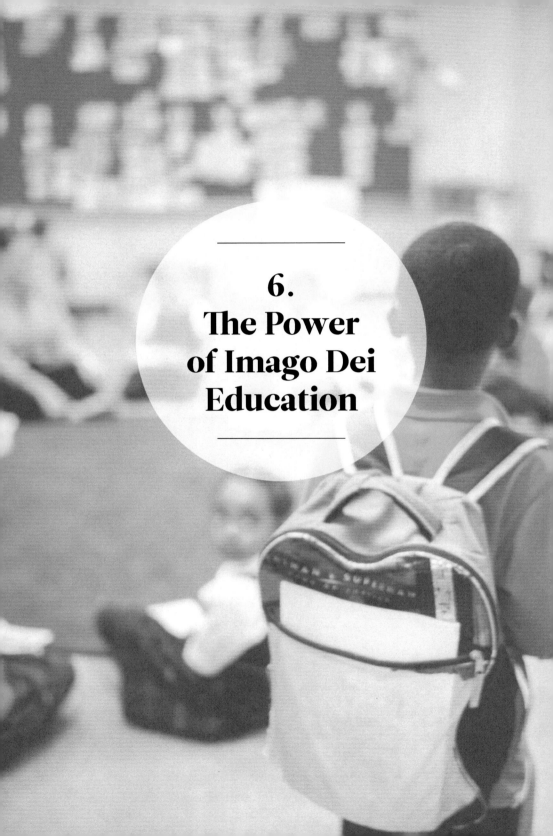

6.
The Power
of Imago Dei
Education

6

A friend of mine, Dr. Vernard Gant, has been an urban school leader for over 30 years. He refers to the students we serve at Hope Academy as ACE Students. It's an acronym meaning students who are <u>A</u>cademically Disenfranchised, <u>C</u>ulturally Diverse, and <u>E</u>conomically Disadvantaged. It's a succinct and memorable way of describing our preferred student.

However, the all-important question is this: Do we see our ACE Students: academically disenfranchised; culturally diverse; and economically disad-vantaged, as children created in the image of God? If the answer is, "Yes," then that means at least three powerful things.

First, it means that our students have a special dignity arising from their bearing the mark of God.

The *imago Dei* means that all children, made according to God's image, are endowed with a dignified status that accords with their connection to Christ the creator. And all children means all children, because it is a status that is conferred by God in creation and not earned or deserved by man.

As Martin Luther King Jr. famously said, "There are no gradations in the image of God. Every man, from the treble white to a bass black is significant on God's keyboard, precisely because every man is made in the image of God."[4]

Throughout history, sinful leaders have perpetrated great evils based on the mistaken idea that there are "gradations" in the image of God—that certain people are more or less deserving of honor than others.

One implication of this in the classroom is unintentionally submitting to a two-tiered approach—especially regarding student expectations. We will trivialize the *imago Dei* in our students if we expect less of some, particularly if they come from an at-risk background. Teachers and Partners at Hope believe that the equal dignity of humanity opens the door for all children to receive a great education.

Second, the *imago Dei* also confers a holy and joyful duty upon all our students—the duty to worship and glorify God. We have all been created with a great and glorious purpose, to reflect the glory of God on the earth. The ultimate purpose of our instruction can never be limited to preparation for college. The ultimate purpose of our instruction must aim higher at what the scriptures call "shalom," or human flourishing according to God's design. As the old catechism puts it, "The chief end of man is to glorify God and enjoy him forever."

The word, "forever," leads to a third massive implication of the *imago Dei*–all of our students have a glorious destiny. As I noted in the C.S. Lewis quote above, we are teaching immortal beings.

---

4. From "The American Dream," a message delivered at Ebenezer Baptist Church, Atlanta, Georgia, on 4 July 1965.

So, how is *imago Dei* education different from other kinds of education practiced in our city? Education for image bearers means that God is exalted at Hope Academy. It means that truth is treasured. It means that parents are involved. It means that teachers are respected and looked to as role models and mentors. It means that students are dignified by high expectations of their behavior and academic work. It means that bullies are disciplined; and achievement gaps are closed; and youth are prepared for college and for a life of God-glorifying work and service.

Imago Dei education means that children will be able to discern the difference between reading *Captain Underpants* and reading *Charlotte's Web*. As image bearers, they will be able to discern what is objectively good and true and beautiful.

Education for image bearers means caring enough about a child to do the really hard work of cultivating virtue and Christ-like character by shepherding student hearts. It means welcoming the immigrant and the stranger God has brought into our city into our school family. And it means not giving up on students, but prayerfully and patiently pursuing God's redemptive work in their lives when they rebel against family and God.

In short, what does *imago Dei* education mean for the youth of our cities?

1. It means that the mis-education of inner-city youth should be one of the most important social justice issues of our day.
2. It means that one of the best strategies to redeem and trans-form under resourced communities is a God-centered school that shapes a generation of wise leaders who love what God loves and hates what God hates.
3. It means that all children are image bearers of God, and so a

school for our neighbors has to be a remarkable school, not just an average one, the kind of school that anyone would want their children to attend.

4. It means that because mankind's chief problem is sin, and because Jesus Christ is the great Savior from sin, a school needs to be based on the gospel and the teachings of Christ.

5. It means that parents shouldn't be ignored, but instead they need to be deeply involved in the solution, and they have to have some real skin in the game.

6. It means it's essential to do the really hard work of holding teachers, parents and students accountable for their responsibilities.

7. It means that results really do matter, and that we have to actually close the achievement gap.

8. Finally, because it's currently against the laws of nearly every state in America to use taxpayer dollars to provide imago Dei education to a child, it means that brothers and sisters living outside the neighborhood will need to help bear the burden and financially partner with inner-city families to make this kind of school affordable for everyone.

For years I continued to disobey God's clear call to start Hope Academy. In 1999, God used my dearest friend, Jeff Bird, as well as a sermon,[5] to give me the courage to quit my job and do something crazy, like starting a school.

Little did Jeff and I know how God would use our little steps of faith to bring hundreds of families, staff, and donors to join us in building a school.

---

5. Piper, John. "The Children of Abraham Are Heirs of the World." desiringGod.org. September 12, 1999.

Today, Hope Academy serves nearly five hundred students in grades kindergarten through twelve, with more than seventy percent of our students eligible for free or reduced price meals. All families sacrifice to pay a "family share" fee, with low income families averaging a fee of eighty dollars a month — no matter how many students are enrolled. In Minneapolis, where we have no parental choice provision, this is possible because hundreds of Partners who give thousands of dollars every year to help a neighbors' child attend our school. We all believe the cause of access to *imago Dei* education is too urgent to wait for policies to change.

We have seen many students beat the odds and become successful beyond our wildest dreams—reading challenging works of literature, studying Latin and Calculus, getting into great colleges, and coming back to our neighborhood to serve our community.[6]

If God might be calling you to bring *imago Dei* education to families in your city, let me end with a warning. Be prepared: the very real burdens, trials, and tragedies of your neighbors will become your own. Fix your eyes on Christ. We always go back to Psalm 127:1:

Unless the LORD builds the house,
those who build it labor in vain.
Unless the LORD watches over the city,
the watchman stays awake in vain.

The image of God. It changed my mind. It changed my heart. And by God's grace it has begun to change the fabric of Minneapolis.

Perhaps God is giving you a vision to take a similar step of faith.

---

6. You can read some of their stories at hopeschool.org/blog/.

Do you have a vision to start a God–centered school in your city?

Become a **Fellow** with Russ Gregg and our team. We help **Fellows** discern their call and experience our model. We equip **Founders** to inspire funders, enroll students, hire staff, train for success and launch your school.

We exist to foster hope in God by kick-starting new God-centered schools in hard places

spreadinghopenetwork.org